MY BLACK KING

By Jean Dancy

Published by InHouse Publishing
Printed in the United States of America.
Cover and interior concept and design: Ava Monroe
Editor: Ava Monroe
ISBN: 9780970277985

To Reach Jean Dancy:
InHouse Publishing
Inhousepublishinginfo@gmail.com
Instagram: @JeanDancy

This book is dedicated to my very own

Black King

my precious husband,

Marty Monroe.

Though you live in heaven now, because of all of the

love and

honor and

respect and

appreciation

that you showered on me daily,

you

inspired me to write this poem.

I love you still...
and I always will.

TABLE OF CONTENTS

Introduction

Dear Black man,

You were made in the image of God. Molded and shaped by HIS hands. You are not an accident or an afterthought. Your place in humanity is **divinely** inspired. Therefore, your presence on Earth is required.

God says, "For I kow that plans I have for you," says The Lord. "They are plans for good and **not** for disaster, to give you a future and a hope."
Jeremiah 29:11 (NLV)

Therefore, **anyone** who comes against you...is coming against God's plan for you.

You are recognized as a lion among men. Some people fear the mere presence of you...long before they get a glimpse of your heart.

You are precious in God's eyes. I want you to see yourself the way God sees you; and I hope my poem is a mirror that will help you do that.

I see you.
I hear you.
I love you.

My Black King

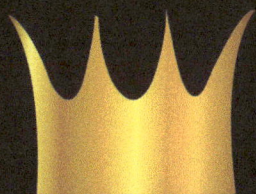

My King

my Black King

Yes, you

The one who survived the winds of hatred that
threatened to blow your pride away

the one who survived the cruel tides that tried to push you back

the one who couldn't be restrained by chains

the one with brakes on your feet
*but you **still** ran, and jumped and soared...*
and roared

NOBODY COULD STOP YOUR LEAP!

the one who braved the storms of racism

the one who waded quicksand to get to me

YOU'RE STILL HERE

After every arrow from hidden bows
couldn't pierce your pride

YOU'RE STILL HERE

When sheet covered midgets weren't tall enough to pull you down

YOU'RE STILL HERE

***You,** the one forced to walk on blood stained soil---from your **OWN** veins*

You, *the one who watched the fruit from your mother's womb---*
hanging from a tree

I honor you
I cherish you

*I will **NOT** bury you*
and I will resurrect every good thing I know
about you

*I will not lift up **My** voice to put you down...*

My King
*My **Black** King*

YES, YOU

The one with the stride
the one America **couldn't** *hide*

We're connected in a way that only scissors from heaven can cut

YOU'RE STILL HERE...

When a million lies couldn't hide the truth
Your *truth*

that you belong where "I" put you

So high...

So high that only God can see you

So high...

So high that only God can show me where you are

So high...

So high that the arms of hatred are too short to reach you

So high...

So high is your palace...in my heart, my King

Your crown is in *My* closet

And I'm ready for the WORLD to see it!

But first

I must show it to you...

my King

I LOVE YOU!

Why did I write this poem?

Question: *What inspired you to write this poem?*

Answer: *My precious husband inspired me to write this poem. Only days after he went to heaven, I sat on the couch thanking God for ever giving him to me. I said, "God, You gave me the man of my dreams...and a marriage that far exceeded anything that I could have ever wanted or imagined."*

Question: *Is that when you wrote it?*

Answer: *Yes, I wrote it that day. I said, "God, I wish I could show all Black men what I feel in my heart right now."*

I thought about all of the obstacles and barriers that Black men go through---just to make it home! I thought about what my grandad went through...and all who survived before him.

Question: *Was it hard to write? I wept as I read it.*

Answer: *It was like giving birth to a baby. Seriously. As a writer, I knew I had to capture the words as they came to me.*

Question: *What do you mean...like giving birth to a baby?*

Answer: *I held my stomach and cried---from the depths of my being as I pushed certain words out...and I wailed and cried to the top of my voice. Then the pain would subside and hit me again like a major constraction. And each time I felt that labor pain---more words poured out of me.*

Question: *How long did it take to write it?*

Answer: *It took hours. When I felt peace and relief...I thought it was over.Then I sat and silent tears ran slowly down my face. My mind traveled through history and I saw some of the atrocities visited upon Black men.*

Question: *Any particular atrocities?*

Answer: *Yes, I saw men hanging from trees and I saw blood stained leaves. I saw cowards covered in sheets because they didn't have the courage to show their faces. The pain came again and stayed until I wrote those words down. It happened over and over. Then like seeing my baby, I felt such joy.*

Question: *Joy?*

Answer: *Yes, I could see how Black men walk in spite of having to walk through hatred.*

*And I started to think about all of the accomplishments that Black men made---**anyway.***

I started to think about how God sees Black men...and how we should see them.

Question: *What do you think your husband would think about this poem?*

Answer: *He would absolutely love it!*

Question: *Is there anything else that you would like to say?*

Answer: *Yes. I hope this poem rings throughout eternity in honor of all Black men.*

About the Auhor

Muhammad Ali fascinated a little girl with his fancy footwork in the ring and caused her to fall in love with the sport of boxing. Her biggest dream was to meet Ali. Though destiny had something even better in mind. That little girl was Jean Dancy.

Author of the poem "My Black King," the Alabama A&M University graduate is grateful to have worked as an Actress, Model, Make- up Artist, Jazz Singer, English Teacher, Sportswriter, Motivational Speaker, Life Skills Teacher, Real Estate Broker, and Certified Mediator.

However, Dancy made Boxing history when she became the only woman to become both a Boxing Manager and a Boxing Promoter. Additionally, Jean is the first female to manage and later promote an athlete who was also her husband. Under Dancy's management, Marty Monroe soared to a #4 world ranking in the Heavyweight boxing division.

Throughout her career, Dancy has received recognition for her achievements. Some of those achievements include being named "Woman of the Year" in sports for her accomplishments in the boxing business and being honored for becoming a member of the multi-million dollar circle of salespeople as a Real Estate Broker.

What about Muhammad Ali?—and destiny?

Jean didn't just meet Ali, she became the only female boxing manager in his Deer Lake Training Camp! Jean has written about her experiences in Ali's camp and her friendship with Muhammad in the riveting book, "Muhammad Ali and Me."

As a Sportswriter, and boxing enthusiast, Dancy has connected with some of the most elite boxers, trainers, and promoters in the history of the sport. That list includes Muhammad Ali, Joe Frazier, George Foreman, Don King, Evander Holyfield, Thomas "Hit Man" Hearns, Roberto Duran, the Mayweathers, and many more.

Jean Dancy, the mother of a lovely daughter named Ava, particularly enjoys helping people in relationships, motivational speaking, singing, and painting.

To Reach Jean Dancy:

InHouse Publishing
Inhousepublishinginfo@gmail.com
Instagram: @JeanDancy
Facebook: Jean Dancy

Please also enjoy...

"Muhammad Ali and Me"
By Jean Dancy

THERE IS NO bigger name or icon on planet Earth than Muhammad Ali (among mere human beings); and despite the odds, God allowed my footsteps to meet at the same place...and at the same time...with his footsteps.

My biggest dream—in life—was to meet Ali, but God had something far greater in mind.

This is the story of a little girl who wanted to meet Muhammad Ali...the lengths she took on that journey...and what happened when her dream finally came true.

Available online at Amazon, Barnes and Noble, and everywhere books are sold.

10 TIPS ON
How to Live a Stress-FREE Life!

By Jean Dancy

10 Tips on How to Live a Stress-FREE Life!

With this book you will learn how to:

- *Start your mornings peacefully*
- *Make yourself a priority*
- *Transcend the stress of traffic*
- *Live life on purpose*

This is a simple book...filled with quick nutritious snacks
that will help you live a healthier and happier life.

Available online at Amazon, Barnes and Noble, and everywhere books are sold.